Baby Precious
Always Shines

Also by Kay Turner

I DREAM OF MADONNA
Women's Dreams of the Goddess of Pop

BETWEEN US
A Legacy of Lesbian Love Letters

BEAUTIFUL NECESSITY
The Art and Meaning of Women's Altars

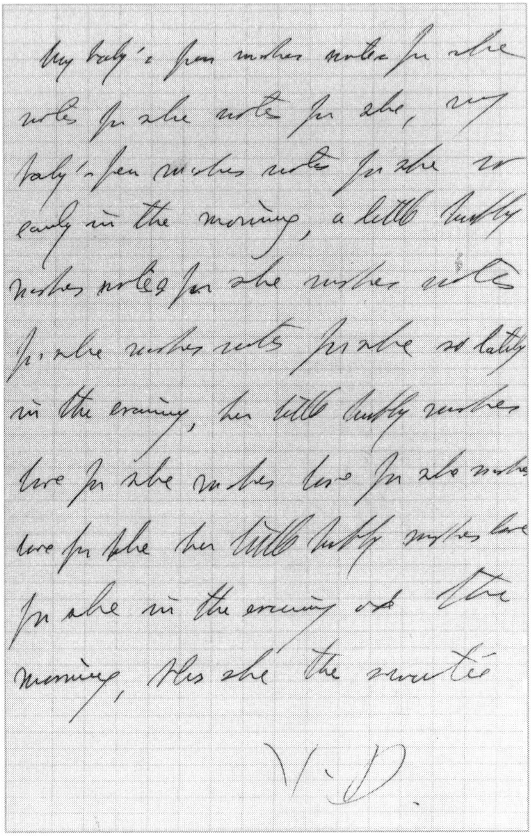

my baby's pen wishes notes for she notes for she notes for she, my baby's pen wishes notes for she so early in the morning, a little hubby wishes notes for she wishes notes for she wishes notes for she so lately in the evening, her little hubby wishes love for she wishes love for she wishes love for she her little hubby wishes love for she in the evening and the morning, bless she the sweetie

St. Martin's Press New York

Baby Precious
Always Shines

Selected Love Notes Between

Gertrude Stein

and

Alice B. Toklas

KAY TURNER

Library of Congress Cataloging-in-Publication Data

Stein, Gertrude, 1874–1946.
    Baby precious always shines : selected love notes between
Gertrude Stein and Alice B. Toklas / [edited] by Kay Turner.—
1st ed.
        p.   cm.
    ISBN 0-312-19832-9
    1. Stein, Gertrude, 1874–1946 Correspondence.   2. Women
authors, American—20th century Correspondence.   3. Lesbians—United States Correspondence.   4. Toklas, Alice B.
Correspondence.   5. Lesbians—France Correspondence.
6. Love letters.   I. Toklas, Alice B.   II. Turner, Kay.
III. Title.
PS3537.T323Z465   1999
818'.5209—dc21
[B]   99-36347
                                                              CIP

First Edition: November 1999

10   9   8   7   6   5   4   3   2   1

This

Book

Is

for

B

Acknowledgments

Many people deserve thanks for their help in bringing this book to publication. For permission to review the original Stein-Toklas notes, I am grateful to Patricia Willis, Curator of the Yale Collection of American Literature. The research staff of the Beinecke Rare Book and Manuscript Library provided patient, professional support. I am especially indebted to Beinecke archivist Timothy G. Young, who diligently, and with keen intelligence, assisted me with transcriptions, clarified historical matters that concern the notes, and generally smoothed the way at various junctures in this project. I thank Beinecke staff members Stephen Jones and Corrina Flanagan, who gave their attention to many of the small details that must be reckoned with in an undertaking such as this one. Several readers of my introduction gave useful comments and critiques. They are Ann Cvetkovich, Ulla Dydo, Belinda Kremer, Hortense Sanger, Mary Sanger, and Timothy G. Young. A version of the introduction was given as a lecture at the University of Winnipeg, and I thank Pauline Greenhill for making possible both that presentation and the stimulating discussion that ensued. Gratitude is also due in great measure to Calman A. Levin, executor of the Gertrude Stein Estate, for permission to publish the notes of Gertrude Stein; to my agent, Cullen Stanley; and to my editor at St. Martin's Press, Michael Denneny, and his assistant, Christina Prestia. The open-door policy and hospitality of the West Ninety-sixth Street gang are gratefully acknowledged. Finally, I give my heart's deepest gratitude to Mary Sanger and Belinda Kremer, without whose love and encouragement this book could not have been written.

This
"Very Beautiful
Form of
Literature"

An Introduction to the Love Notes Between
Gertrude Stein and Alice B. Toklas

Baby precious sweet and mine, baby
precious all the time, baby precious
darling wife I do love with all
my life, baby precious tender and
true, little hubby is all for you,
baby precious lovely wife baby
precious sweet my wife, dear
baby

Y.D.

[2920–42]

1

Gertrude Stein met Alice B. Toklas in September 1907. Toklas began typing manuscripts for her in 1908, and by 1909 she was a part of the Stein household and on her way to becoming an everlasting partner in Stein's life. Alice moved into 27, rue de Fleurus in 1910 and there, after the less than amicable departure of Stein's brother, Leo, in 1913, she and Gertrude made their famous home together. As Stein asserted in "If You Had Three Husbands," "They had likeness. Likeness to what. Likeness to loving," and "It happened very simply that they were married. They were naturally married."[1] Their "likeness to loving"—as well as their profound difference—inspired a marriage that remained in force and indefatigable for thirty-nine years, until Stein's death in 1946.

Much has been written about the relationship between Gertrude Stein and Alice B. Toklas. It has been said that Stein's every effort to transcend and transform Western literature was predicated on her love for Toklas, and because this love was so central to Stein's achievement, arguments abound that seek to capture or illuminate the Stein-Toklas alliance. Many portray the relationship as unequal, with Stein clearly assuming the superior status of "masculine" genius, artist, and mentor and Toklas occupying the "feminine," subordinate position of secretary, cook, and willing servant. Writing in the 1980s, feminists such as Shari Benstock described and somewhat resentfully critiqued Stein and Toklas for imitating heteronormative patterns of dominance and domesticity. In the 1990s, lesbian writers, including Elizabeth Meese and Esther Newton, countered this critique by recuperating the butch-femme terms of the coupling, which femme philosopher Joan Nestle calls "complex erotic statements, not phony heterosexual replicas."[2] Biographers have offered psychological motivations for the relationship. Diana Souhami, for example, sees it as a prophylactic against emotional pain. She suggests that Gertrude's pre-Alice entanglement in a devastating love triangle gave rise to her "theory of obligation" and the wish to find a mutually satisfying and long-lasting monogamous partnership.[3]

Yes, Stein and Toklas have the reputation of being the most famous lesbian couple of the twentieth century. Much about them has been conjectured, and each version of the relationship's raison d'être is fueled by what Stein and Toklas said and did not say about their love for each other. Certainly they wrote of their relationship in published works such as Stein's *The Autobiography of Alice B. Toklas*, *Ada*, *Lifting Belly*, and *Tender Buttons* and Toklas's memoir *What Is Remembered*. Informally, it was spoken of in their correspondence with others and in innumerable anecdotes—whether true or not—told and written about them by those who knew them during their lifetime. A story recorded by their young gay friend Samuel Steward finds Stein speaking to him casually of her lesbian alliance with Toklas, even inviting him to write about it, but not "for twenty years after I die, unless it's found out sooner, or times change."[4]

Thankfully, times *have* changed, and yet for all we now know or assume about Gertrude and Alice's relationship, we know little of the actual workings of their marriage as they created it just between themselves on a daily basis for decades. Fortunately—perhaps even fatefully—there exists a small collection of documents that inscribe the innermost reality of the marriage.

Off and on, during the entire period they were together, Gertrude and Alice wrote each other little love notes. Because the two were virtually inseparable, the notes were written and read at home in Paris, first at 27, rue de Fleurus, later at 5, rue Christine, and at their summer home at Bilignin in southeastern France. Calling her "wifey" and most often addressing her as "baby precious," Stein penned her love for Toklas in warm words of adoration and unself-conscious desire. Almost without exception, she signed herself "Y.D.," short for "Your Darling." Her notes are the small but significant testimonies to her long-lived love for the "wife" who was also her "birdie," her "sweetie," her "boss," her "little ball," and her "treasure." Toklas responded in kind, declaring her devotion in dispatches to her "husband," whom she also called "lovie," "baby boy," "Mr. Pottie," "sweet pinky," and "Mr. Cuddlewuddle."

Baby Precious Always Shines presents examples from this previously unpublished correspondence. In first-person documentation, in direct address, these little notes—brief though they are—disclose the intimacies of a deeply committed, very rare, and at the same time very ordinary marriage. They render in domestic ephemera an "autobiography" of the union between Alice B. Toklas and Gertrude Stein.

Bringing these notes to print now, in an age that thrives on the public exposure of private lives, raises certain issues of responsibility. The notes are revelatory; they do unveil secrets, and I have struggled—anxiously at times—over whether or not certain of these secrets should be told. Still, no truth exposed here concerns anything except the power of love, expressed in a particular way between two women. And nothing here has not been revealed—even if at times obliquely—by

Interior of 27, rue de Fleurus; photo dated 1920 in Toklas's handwriting.

Stein herself in her literary works. The notes and the writing, the life and the art, are intimately linked.

I came to this project not as a Stein scholar, but as a lesbian reader and admirer of Stein's work and as a folklorist interested in the history and traditions of gay culture. I was first told about the Stein-Toklas love notes while researching my edited collection *Between Us: A Legacy of Lesbian Love Letters,* published in 1996. That book, which includes material from both famous and unknown lovers, valorizes the historical lesbian love letter as an often defiantly written, rarely preserved, and yet decisive document that certifies the enduring vitality and variation of our desire. My interest in publishing the Stein-Toklas correspondence follows the same logic; now the love notes of Gertrude Stein and Alice B. Toklas may take their place in the published history of a literary art that began with Sappho almost three thousand years ago. Moreover, these notes are, I think, a necessary addition to the corpus of Stein's published works. If the vast outpouring of her accomplishment was fostered in the domestic bliss of her marriage to Toklas, the presentation of these notes achieves the particular power of illuminating that accomplishment with direct evidence of its inspiration.

The complete collection of a little over three hundred notes—two hundred ninety-five from Gertrude and seventeen from Alice—is housed in the Gertrude Stein and Alice B. Toklas Papers in the Yale Collection of American Literature at the Beinecke Rare Book and Manuscript Library at Yale University. They are filed under an intriguing title, "Autrespondence" (in French, *autre* means "other"), although the reason for the designation and who gave it are unknown. Most of the notes are less than a hundred words long, and not a single one is dated. Many can be tentatively identified as having been written in the early years of the relationship, but passing remarks concerning specific historical events suggest that a majority originated in the years 1935–1946, by which time the relationship had aged to its own kind of perfection.[5] The charm of these notes is found in the romance of the ordinary, in the domestic routine of loving long and well.

Under the aegis of Donald Gallup, then the curator of the Yale Collection of American Literature, Stein began giving her manuscripts and notebooks to the library for safekeeping in 1937, during the early years of World War II in Europe. In 1947, not long after Stein's death, Toklas sent the library most of Stein's remaining manuscripts, notebooks, and correspondence. Along with these came numerous bits and pieces— receipts, recipes, photos, calling cards, invitations, and so on—that traced the couple's cherished domestic life. The love notes were provided to the Beinecke at this time, too, but by all accounts, they were given by mistake. When Gallup apprised Toklas of her unintended gift, she at first insisted that the stray notes be destroyed, then relented with a demand that they not be made publicly available. The notes were put in a locked cabinet until 1981, when the library decided to make them accessible for research. In 1995 they were officially catalogued for inclusion in the Stein-Toklas corpus.[6]

The consummately private Toklas probably never intended their publication, yet certainly she recognized the value of intimate notes as tokens of love's veracity. She had, after all, saved them for years. In fact, it seems that a number of the notes may have been composed in response to her specific request for them. One of her memos to Stein says, in part: "Notes are a very beautiful form of literature; they are never too frequent, do not fear to overwhelm me with the[m]" [2929–9]. From Alice's point of view, this "very beautiful form of literature" most particularly infixed Gertrude's love, passion, and concern for her. Stein's primary labors as a writer were inspired by Toklas but aimed outward to the world, and in competition, no less, with the male-dominated avant-garde of the period. These little leavings of dedication and desire— in effect the unofficial marriage contract regularly, if casually, renewed—were destined for Toklas alone.

Stein was known to follow a regimen of writing late into the night, and probably most of her notes were written at the end of these work sessions. She quite regularly mentions that she has "worked a little" or "a lot" and is now "getting sleepy" and thinking about joining her "wifey" in bed. Right before retiring, she left her midnight missives for Alice, an early riser, to find as she began her day. No doubt prized as little treasures, the notes were discovered in various places throughout the house; their contents suggest, for example, that some were interleaved in manuscripts Alice was transcribing, while others were left in the bedroom or bathroom.

A typical note from Stein reads:

Baby precious Hubby worked and
loved his wifey, sweet sleepy wifey,
dear dainty wifey, baby precious sleep
sweetly and long is hubby's song,
and all mine and sweet is hubby's
treat and precious and true and all
for you is hubby   Y.D.
[2926–13]

At the level of composition, the notes follow the word-inverted, long-breathed, rolling, repetitive, refluent style that Stein invented and gave to the world in many of her published works. They are written in Gertrude's lazy, loopy scrawl or once in a while in a cramped, tiny version of the same, on squared graph paper or sometimes on available scraps of watercolor paper, on frontispieces ripped from the dime novels Gertrude read for pleasure, or on the dark blue stationery headed in tiny block letters with their address at Bilignin. The paper used—whether half-sheet or full, lined or unlined, notebook or stationery, raggedly torn portion or complete sheet—in large part determines the notes' lineation. Brief, mantralike enticements, Stein's notes are variously tender and beseeching, caring and confessing, funny and gamesome, sexually charged and sincere, quotidian and queer, and always passionate. Each one marks the pleasures—infrequently, the pains—of married love.

Repeated themes and other similarities between some of the notes indicate that a number of them were written in se-

Rent receipt for 27, rue de Fleurus, dated October 15, 1936.

ries, perhaps two or three in the same night or over the course of a few days. One series extols the erotic virtues of cigarettes; another celebrates the joys of writing endearments on a fresh graph-lined pad. Images seen in Stein's formal works also find their way into the notes, or may have been first conceived in writing them. The famously obscure "Caesars" are here, as well as the infamous "cows." Scholars and devotees of Stein will find especially interesting the correspondences in tropes, diction, and themes between her formal and informal writing.

Stein was, of course, the more prolific writer in the duo, but Alice's recordings, even though more occasional, are equally enticing. Jotted in her well-formed, precise script, Alice's notes by turns express desire, adoration, and yearning, but they are also given to a wickedly humorous and seductive chastisement of her "hubby." Several consciously imitate and parody Stein's unpunctuated, repetitive style: "Baby boy /

9

You're no toy / But a strong-strong husband / I dont [*sic*] obey"
[2929–2].

Eight of Toklas's notes are typed. Here we find her grumbling about the need to practice her typing, yet seemingly untroubled by making loads of mistakes as she informs "Mr. Pottie" that although she is a bit behind in her transcription work, she is still giving "him" an "industrious wife's devotion," and she reminds "him": "Please be sure not to forget that you are the most illustrious / and distinguished husband a [*sic*] an industrious wife ever had" [2929–11]. In another typed memo, likely passed directly to Gertrude, Alice writes that she has "just looked / up to see if you were as beautiful as I re-memvered [*sic*] and I found / that you were employed with a pencul [*sic*] and paper" [2929–9]. The Alice we discover in lines such as these is witty and ironic, temperamental but tempting, devoted yet disobedient.

We tend to think of Gertrude as large—large in body, in life, and in art—but she made herself small for Alice. She became a "little king" for her "happy queen" [2924–18] or a "little hubby" who "will do / what he is told / by little wifey" [2919–14]. Alice, though praised for her physical diminutiveness—her "little face" [2921– 17] and her "little nose" [2925–36]—was the bigger force, in Gertrude's eyes: "she is so wonderfully she / and he is only a little he" [2925–42].

When fitted together, the notes create a tantalizing mosaic of a marriage between two women that was built to last. Its longevity was based in heterosexual convention—one being husband, the other wife—but here convention was never saddled with acquiescence or denial; rather, it was fully chosen and manipulated for the purposes of pleasure and freedom. Although written with a different intent, a telling statement Stein makes in *Paris France* suggests the degree to which she likely understood her and Alice's appropriation of heterosexual norms as a distinct advantage: "I cannot write too much upon how necessary it is to be completely conservative that is particularly traditional in order to be free."[7]

In terms of their relationship, to be conservative, to be married, to be husband and wife was not about the imitation of heterosexual, bourgeois privilege; it was about the erotic cadence found in the central enjoyment of habit and repetition. "To be free" was, for Gertrude and Alice, to fully embrace the primary energy of recapitulation that marriage affords.

Early on, in *The Making of Americans*—the book she was working on when she met Toklas and began their relationship; also the first book Alice typed for her—Stein underscored the critical import of repetition as the driving force in coming "to feel the whole of anyone":

> When you come to feel the whole of anyone from the beginning to the ending, all the kind of repeating there is in them, the different ways at different times repeating comes out of them, all the kinds of things and mixtures in each one, anyone can see then by looking hard at any one living near them that a history of every one must be a long one. A history of any one must be a long one, slowly it comes out from them from their beginning to their ending, slowly you can see it in them the nature and the mixtures in them, slowly everything comes out from each one in the kind of repeating each one does in the different parts and kinds of living they have in them, slowly then the history of them comes out from them, slowly then any one who looks well at any one will have the history of the whole of that one.[8]

Whether or not she had Toklas in mind as she wrote this passage, Stein perfectly captures here the essence of their marriage. As her wife, Alice became Gertrude's ideal lifetime subject for "A history of any one," for "the different ways . . . repeating comes out of them," for "all the kinds of things and mixtures in each one."[9] As husband, Gertrude became the "any one who looks well at any one," who was Alice.

Within the marriage, the art of "looking well" was embedded in repetition. Repetition required a constant milieu, which was provided within the close quarters of home. In this interior, preserved by Alice, the habitual created a haven. As Shari Benstock suggests, the couple's domestic life was crucial to Stein's art because it "established a boundary of significant experience, a separate, interior space" that shielded her from "the world of patriarchal power outside the walls of her apartment."[10]

The notes are filled with the mundane details of Toklas and Stein's "significant experience" of living together. Day by day, the accumulation of the ordinary lent inspiration to Stein's writing and added weight to the couple's commitment. Gertrude reports that she has "cut off ivy off the / terrace," [2925–18] or "cleaned up and oiled your scissors, / and so was a little useful" [2920–45]. She attempts to remedy a typical household crisis, saying, "I been all / through your desk so you do not have to / worry about that, and I did not find the ticket," but eventually, "I found the ticket in your bag" [2920–18]. She reports on their dogs, the little Chihuahua named Pepe and the beloved poodles, Basket, who died in 1938, and Basket II: "Basket is barking and we will go to bed," [2918–15] or "Basket and me played" [2922–27]. A singular moment of bad behavior on the poodle's part provokes this warning: "My precious, be careful not / to slip on the floor down- / stairs because Basket has been / hunting slabs of butter every / where" [2924–15]. The vigilance required to avoid the assaults of cold, wet weather is regularly mentioned. Gertrude often records that she has been out "sawing wood" for the fire. In one note she thanks Toklas for buying her a raincoat, "a so beautiful blue impermeable" [2925–47]; in another, she jokes about the "hotties" (hot water bottles) used to warm their bed [2920–24].

The notes celebrate seasonal events such as birthdays, Christmas, and New Year's. They also refer to historical events of the period that had a direct effect on the couple's life. Gertrude and Alice went through the harrowing circumstances of both world wars, yet, as Stein asserts, their commitment was only deepened—never undone—by the crises: "I love you so much more / every war more and more and more and / more" [2925–49]. The turbulence of the times could always be buffered by the intimate accord discovered in the simple enjoyment of domestic rituals: "by loveing [sic] / her flowers and her food / I tell my wifey how I / love her, yes I do" [2928–17].

Ultimately, the dailiness of their life together was devoted to Stein's literary endeavors. If a muse is a visiting spirit who inspires an artist and then disappears, Alice was not a muse. She never disappeared. More like Hestia, the Greek goddess of primal conjugality, Alice was the keeper of the hearth flame. The fire she watched, fed, banked, and never let go out was Gertrude's.

The notes attest to this constancy, and to the degree to which Stein relied on it. Many of them include reports on the status of her current work. She announces on the day of finishing *Ida:* "The story of Ida / Finis" [2919–2]. After a long night of reading and commenting on a manuscript, she says she will show it to Alice and further proclaims:

> . . . Ill [*sic*] show everything to my wifey, all me all
>   everything
> because I am all hers blessed blessed wifey,
> so beautiful so tender so true and I am
> all you, blessed dear blessed wifey, I
> am all filled with love for you all
> filled up with love of you nothing in
> me but love of you my wifey true
> my tender sweet wifey my lovely
> wifey I am all you and you are all
> me . . .
> **[2918–15]**

Stein trusted Toklas as her mirror and as the best audience for her work. In effect, Toklas *was* the work. Elizabeth Meese explains, "Stein could not have given us her lesbian: writing without Alice B. Toklas—not because of the feeding, tending, and typing, but because of loving her, constructing her as the site of composition."[11]

In another instance Gertrude has just completed her labors on an unnamed volume and says to Alice, "bless the baby whatever I / do only makes me love her / more bless the baby the / sweet the perfect the precious / baby" [2923–6]. Writing spurs loving; loving spurs writing. Stein quantifies her artistic output as a measure of her love for Toklas; her engagement in the art of writing is commensurate with the act of loving:

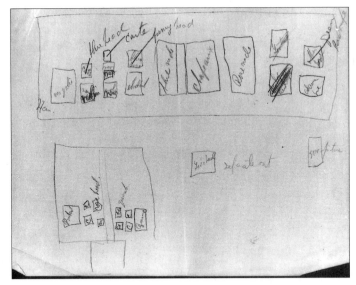

Sketch for wall placement of the famed painting collection at 27, rue de Fleurus, October 1914.

Precious baby I had an attack
of working and I wrote lots of
pages and I loved my blessed
wifie so completely so
entirely that even dear sweet
precious wifey is satisfied with
all the love with which I love
her . . .
[2923–7]

Gertrude's stamina in writing—her nocturnal burning of
words onto the page—is likened to sexual stamina, to going the

distance to satisfy Alice. Alice's response is seductive in its approval and encouragement; a "morning-after" note from her begins: "Sweet / pinky / You made / lots of literature / last night didn't / you. It is very good. I / like this one best. You are doing most hand- / somely" [2929–7].

Erotic and sexual energy drive the work and the marriage, and this is playfully inscribed in the many references implicitly linking love, sex, and writing through the metaphor of the pen or pencil: "I use the little goldy pencil / to tell my sweet love she is my / life, I use the little goldy / pencil to tell her I love / but her" [2924–20]. As her use of the "little goldy pencil" suggests, Gertrude loved the physicality of writing her love for Alice; it implies, too, that she loved the physicality of making love to her. In another example, the pen serves as the symbolic analogue for rendering her desire:

> Baby precious, the pen seems to
> be writing beautifully and not
> blotting at all, I thought it was
> because it was not full enough,
> I think it blots when it needs filling,
> and my baby needs filling with love
> every second and she is she is
> she is filled up full every
> second, . . .
> [2922–39]

Stein stole the crudely overdetermined cliché of the phallic pen and rewrote it as an instrument of lesbian-made love and art. That long-exclusive metaphor for heterosexual male creativity is employed by Stein at times rompishly, at times endearingly. What's more, the pen she refers to is just as often

Alice's: "My dearest wife, / This little pen which / belongs to you loves to be / written by me for you, its [sic] / never in a stew nor are / you my sweet ecstacy [sic]" [2921–5a].

There is something lustily contradictory and compelling, something really quite revolutionary, in the notion of this symbolic phallus being controlled by two women. Between them, they used the propagating potential of the pen to affirm their union and, as married couples do, to make babies—in the form of Stein's literary productions. In one note Gertrude fills up Alice's fountain pen and proceeds to have "lots and lots and lots of babies, nice babies for / my baby, bless my baby, nice babies / for my blessed baby" [2922–21].

Together Gertrude and Alice embrace the ecstasy of their inversion. They also imaginatively subvert and convert the conventions of conjugal love to suit their own pleasures and creativity. Gertrude is not always or necessarily the "male" who uses "his" pen to make "babies." "He" sometimes uses "her" pen—Alice's "phallus," her inspirational power—to fertilize the womb of "his" art.

Nor does the masculine "pen" hold sway. Here it is traded for the feminine "page" in a gentle proclamation of desire:

. . . She is a tender page
and every page is open to
me and every page in me
is open to she . . .
[2925–45]

Moreover, Stein moves beyond the "masculine" and the "feminine," populating her erotic lexicon with gender-free symbols. Her desire for "baby precious" is called up in describing her as "tender as the / fall and lovely as a wall" [2928–10], or in associating her with the color blue [2925–8] or with numbers: "One two three and in all three is / all my love for she baby precious" [2927– 11]. Stein's sense of the erotic was essentially nondiscriminatory.

Judy Grahn says that Stein questions "our very basic patterns of relationship, at the level of linguistic relationship."[12] The Stein-Toklas marriage engaged a politics of sexual and gender anarchy, abetted by linguistic anarchy. Central to much of what queer culture and lesbian-feminist theory have given us in the past two decades—from drag kings to gay genes, from Joan Nestle to Judith Butler, from recent legal considerations of gay marriage to newly reconfirmed butch-femme roles—is a radical reconstruction of gender. What it means to be male or female, masculine or feminine, gay or straight, husband or wife, is open now to more flexible interpretation. Yet the love notes of Stein and Toklas demonstrate that they were way ahead of our late-twentieth-century project of revising, improvising, and revolutionizing gendered categories.

Certainly Gertrude was always "hubby" and Alice was always "wifey," but they used male and female standards not as dyes or molds but as templates, which could be repositioned and refired, day by day, night by night, in the domestic kiln of their radical love. They assumed their roles with a knowing touch of camp.

Kate Bornstein suggests that camp is the "leading edge in the deconstruction of gender" because it "reclaims gender and re-shapes it as a consensual game."[13] Stein and Toklas reveled in a kind of domestic theatricality; they staged the gendered roles of husband and wife as an obvious yet meaningful performance—a form of "serious play." An early and relatively unknown piece of Stein's called "Play" opens: "Play, play every day, play and play and play away, and then play the play you played to-day, the play you play every day, play it and play it. Play it and remember it and ask to play it."[14] Toklas was, of course, Stein's favorite playmate, and their favorite game was the marriage they made every day by playing it, remembering it, and asking to play it. Repeatedly, their notes convey this with a sense of knowing glee and the freedom of an intimate in-joke. Over and over again, Gertrude professes her role as deeply admiring yet somewhat hapless husband:

Baby precious,
       My eyes are getting sleepy and my love is
getting strong and now in a few minutes I
will be coming along to climb in nice and quiet
and not make baby cross because cold air comes
in to win a little scolding from my boss, bless
wifee
[2918-11]

Meanwhile, Alice in her notes plays the part of attentive but admonishing wife:

. . . Hubby must
not worry but ask Marie
to tell me to come up to
make your coffee. Be
rested and all loving &
know wifie thinks you
are better behavioured
every second . . .
[2929-4]

19

In marriage, playfulness with language—codes, nick-names, neologisms—is a source of the bonding that keeps the marriage active, alive. No one knew this better than Gertrude and Alice. Theirs was a paradigm of the way language play invents and sustains intimate relationships.

Yet the theater of Gertrude and Alice's gender performance is never just rhetorical. Such performance ultimately served to create erotic tension. These two women chose conventional heterosexual markers, "husband" and "wife," to name the decidedly sexual core of their marriage. The notes quite explicitly document the physical pleasures of their union. Gertrude's late-night reveries often reflect bodily urgencies, her desire to satisfy and be satisfied. She gets sleepy after working "a little" and "wants to come / up and cuddle next" to Alice, whom she describes as "warm," "tasty," and "smelly" [2927-13].

On a cold night she says it is "not so cold that I am not . . . / loveing [sic] my baby wife, my precious / darling sweet desirable baby wife, and / she needs me and I need she and we / are as loving as loving can be" [2920-38]. She obviously enjoyed the married privilege of sleeping with her wife. Bedtime was Stein's reward for work accomplished, and she often took her prize physically: "I am very sleepy now and I am going to go / to sleep sweetly kissing my wifey bless her" [2924-4].

Note after note records the expectation that kisses will be given regularly, night and day, always: "she will sleep tight and / to-morrow morning she will be / longing for what for a kiss oh yes" [2921-2]. The result of kissing is married harmony; kissing is the way Gertrude wins Alice over and over again: "And what will she say / when they kiss to-day / she will say he is a good / little boysy" [2921-9]. Kissing is also a sign of possession, making her hers. Gertrude's overwhelming urge to kiss Alice often expresses itself in rapturous litanies of love and lust. In one example, she covers Alice with kisses, repeatedly affirming her "complete" and "everlasting" love:

> . . . I kiss you dear blessed wifey
> I kiss you again dear blessed wifey
> I kiss you again and again dear blessed wifey
> I kiss you again and again and again dear blessed wifey
> I just completely and entirely and everlastingly love
> you dear
> blessed wifey

[2925–52]

Gertrude's relish in kissing Alice is the most direct evidence of their physical passion, but it is in no way its limit. Lap-sitting seems to have played its part in providing erotic stimulation. Describing Alice in one note as "the nicely heavy / on the knee" [2920–44], Stein says in another: "My baby is a birdie sitting on a / bough, and the bough is hubby" [2926–1]. Several of the notes implicate hands and fingers in a sexual way. In an example such as "My fingers is stiff my love is / strong, my baby is my darling just / right along" [2925–7], Stein's fingers may have been stiff from writing or from the cold, but they were also stiff with desire. The double entendre was probably not lost on Alice.

Other passages exalt consummation. An obscure note seems to laud the "glue" of sexual lubrication: "How are we tight / Glue is our delight, / What silky, / Yes milky / Dear legs all alright" [2925–5]. And in another, Stein records her enthusiasm for:

. . . The darling. This
ejaculation refers to Mrs. not to Mr.
as might be erroneously supposed.
Mrs. is the fountain of all good
all beauty and all sweetness. Mrs.
is a graceful fountain and she
plays over Mr. who is certain that
Mrs. is a grateful fountain . . .
[2921–3]

I venture to say that Alice, the "graceful" and "grateful fountain," apparently preempted recent claims for the possibility of female ejaculation. This fastidious, taciturn, and at times sharp-tongued "Mrs." obviously had and gave her pleasures. Here she remarks on sexually satisfying Gertrude with the same regularity as feeding her: "wifie's good / Hides it under a thick hood / It will be your constant food / Good baby / Is all me / To delight / With all my might / Hubby is my pleasure" [2929–2].

Stein once ranted that "the nineteenth century is dead dead dead," and several writers have claimed that she helped kill it by inventing new and noncanonical ways to use language.[15] As the notes strongly indicate, the Stein-Toklas relationship also killed the nineteenth century in a specifically lesbian way. From its very beginnings, their physically active marriage disclaimed the putatively asexual era of romantic friendship between women. Theirs was never a futile nor a frustrated love.

They outdid their lesbian contemporaries as well. While Radclyffe Hall fretted neurotically over her "inversion," and Vita Sackville-West tried to have it both ways, remaining heterosexually wed to Harold Nicholson and at the same time

22

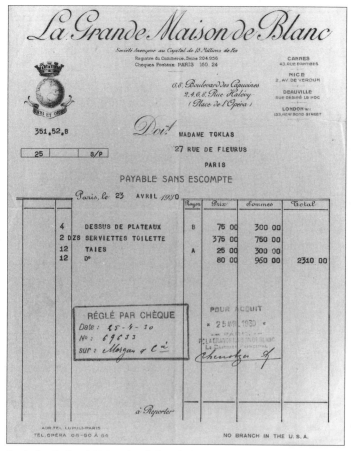

Receipt from La Grande Maison Blanc for household linens purchased by Toklas.

wreaking homo-havoc in her love affairs with women, Gertrude and Alice simply married, set up house, had sex, and stayed together, mostly for better, rarely for worse. Pleasing their pleasure was the measure of everything they did, and it was accomplished most effectively by both claiming and subverting matrimonial convention for their own purposes. In fact, their marriage was played in the very realm where the subversion of heterosexual norms is most feared. Gertrude and Alice claimed both the sexual terms and the domestic benefits of being husband and wife. They did not have an affair or a romantic friendship or a partnership; they had a marriage—made perhaps in heaven, but made most certainly on earth.

There are, of course, the recorded admissions of failure to love well enough. A few of Gertrude's notes ask forgiveness for being "naughty" or "hurtful." Sometimes jealousy is implied, but whatever the cause of these momentary lapses, Stein is always anxious to return the marriage to a steady state: "My darling wifey, I am so sorry I was / so hurtful and I love my wife so and I / am all hersy and nobody elses [*sic*] only my / wifey's, I adore you wifey . . ." [2924–12]. She vows:

> . . . I must not
> upset me which is to upset she
> not for anything and so baby can see
> that I will not upset he because
> that is to upset she, and little she
> and little me must not upset she . . .
> [2920–5]

Disruption of the couple's devotion was unacceptable.

If the notes provide an inside view of the physical privileges of the Stein-Toklas marriage, they also, in a quite remarkably revelatory way, give evidence contradictory to the assumption that many commentators have made concerning how such privilege was symbolized in Stein's literary works.

For years feminists and lesbians, scholars and admirers—including me—have claimed "cows" as Stein's code for lovemaking, or more specifically for Toklas's orgasms.

The insinuating carnality of "cows" crops up in many of Stein's writings; early, for example, in "Lifting Belly" (written between 1915 and 1917) and in "As A Wife Has A Cow A Love Story" (written in 1923). Both works are often cited as indicative of the couple's sexual relationship. A brief excerpt from the latter shows why:

> Have it as having having it as happening, happening
> to have it as having, having to have it as happening. . . .
> and my wife has a cow as now, my wife having a cow as
> now, my wife having a cow as now, my wife having a cow
> as now and having a cow . . . and having a cow now, . . .[16]

Any reader, especially a lesbian reader, might tilt toward the orgasmic implications of a wife "having a cow now." It seems certain, however, from the love notes that "cow" has a double meaning, or a singularly different meaning from that which previously has been attributed to it.

The most startling revelation in the notes comes from what may be for some a troubling realm, the scatological. I paraphrase Yeats, her contemporary, in saying that at least in part, Stein "pitched [her] mansion" of love for Toklas "in the place of excrement."[17] More than a third of the notes demonstrate unequivocally that "cows" are Toklas's feces or stools, as Stein defines them in one example: "And / what is a stool. That was / the elegant name for a cow" [2921–8]. In the 1970s, writers on Stein and Toklas such as Richard Bridgman and Linda Simon veered toward this understanding, yet they pulled back—out of a sense of propriety, disbelief, or repulsion—from claiming that the loving command for a "cow" from Alice is the command for a bowel movement:

> . . . I love my
> wifey so completely oh so completely,
> and, she is to have a lovely cow, a real
> cow splash goes the cow now, splash
> splash splash. Lovely baby smelly cow comes
> out of baby anyhow now, . . .
> [2918–3]

Another note, equally definitive, reads:

> When this you see sweetly and slowly out
> from she will splash from her little behind
> just nicely plop into the water . . .
> out comes a cow . . .
> [2918–5]

Perhaps the term derives from Gertrude and Alice's slightly altered definition of the locution "to have a cow," meaning to have a fit or spasm, or from their revamping of the elocutionary exercise "how now brown cow," or from some joke they shared about "cow pies" or "cow patties," euphemisms that have been in the American lexicon for a long time. Whatever the usage's origin between them, Stein coded the true meaning of "cows" in her formal writing by rarely qualifying or describing them. Occasionally she gave a clue—the "elegant stool" definition actually appears, word for word, in "Vacation in Brittany"[18]—but, generally, she left her readers to imagine what "cows" were, and many of us have imagined

Alice's orgasms. Writing to Alice alone, however, Stein characterized "cows" explicitly.

Now, it could be that she purposefully confounded the orgasmic and the excretory expulsions of Alice's body, but the notes rarely suggest so. Orgasms are not "smelly," nor do they go "splash" or "plop." They are not shaped like a "banana" [2927–9]. It is the anus that yields the "cow."

Certainly, Gertrude's repeated command that Alice produce a "cow" begs for interpretation. In purely pragmatic terms, the loving command reflects the degree to which Stein was Toklas's caretaker as much as Toklas was Stein's. Many of Gertrude's notes express general concern over Alice's health and welfare. In one, she says with relief, "I am so happy that my / baby's little aches and pains / is better so much better" [2920–49]. In another, she advises, "Baby precious, must not work too hard, / must not baby precious must be taken / care of by hubby" [2926–5].

The "cow" notes refer specifically to the likelihood that Alice suffered a digestive condition, perhaps the painfully ironic result of her culinary acumen or just the demon of her particular physical constitution. The problem may have been spastic colon, severe indigestion, or general constipation. No diagnosis is given, but whatever the cause, Stein doctored the problem through a variety of what she called "treatments" to produce a "cow." Some of these are described; in one note she documents feeding Alice an apple and giving her a tablespoonful of medicine [2922–49]; in a second, she urges that drinking tea and mineral water "will cure my baby / now" and ends, "we love each other / oh so much be well / my baby at my touch" [2919–10].

More often, though, Stein gave her healing "touch" in "treatments" that were purely mental and linguistic; they were in effect *en*treatments. She solicits "cows" by writing them into existence. She "concentrates" on her wife's cow [2922–30]; she does "so earnestly treat and pray" [2923–4] that her wife will have a cow. A remarkably candid series of notes was written in succession "to help squeezy / the sweet smelly cow out of she" [2922–9], "to make it come / through the splendid little behind / of my precious beloved" [2922–8]. And in parallel with the actual cigarettes Alice may have smoked to induce a bowel movement, Gertrude becomes the fanciful cigarette that will stimulate the release of a cow:

> Baby precious, kisses and hugs make
> baby know that her cigarette works and
> is a cigarette just as often as she
> needs it, bless the baby she needs
> it now, baby is smoking her little
> hubby now and the result is
> a lovely cow, no pains no aches
> no behind troubles at all but just
> a lovely easy smelly cow now . . .
> [2922–34]

Finally, and most endearingly, she uses her love for Alice to produce a cow: "How I love you, baby precious, I love / you so much that a cow will come out" [2922–6]. Gertrude's demand for "cows" is perhaps no more and no less than a well-meaning and devoted "husband's" concern for her wife's comfort. In fact, this concern is often inscribed with deep tenderness:

> Blessed Baby,
> Baby is all warm

Coffee is all warm
Bath is all warm
Cow coming out of
little behind is all
warm
And baby is free from harm
[2925-2]

Stein's attention to Toklas's bowel movements exemplifies, in a profound sense, the hallmark of married intimacy: one body entrusted to another, singularly known, cared for, loved, and desired in all its intricacies, all its successes—and all its failings. In any long-lasting union—and I think most married readers would agree—love expresses itself daily in rituals of bodily caretaking. That Stein was so sympathetically engaged with Toklas regarding her "regularity" surely indicates the depth of her commitment to "love, honor and cherish" Alice "in sickness and in health."

Alice may have had the more temperamental constitution, but Gertrude suffered her physical setbacks as well. A few of the notes serve as responses to "treatments" given by Alice to Gertrude: "I sawed wood hard and that and my baby's / treatment has made me all well" [2925-37]. There is no doubt that the Stein-Toklas marriage was traditionally corporeal in its concerns.

I would add, too, that the couple lived during the period that saw the rise of the "cult of regularity," a popular health craze encouraging unembarrassed discussion and monitoring of bowel movements. In one note, a gentle requirement is made for a movement at a specific time in the morning: "my baby precious is going to / have a nice movement come out at eight / o clock [sic] just like her hubby has, fine / says hubby

fine that dear wifey has / such a nice movement come out"
[2927–16]. Both Toklas's and Stein's regular "movements"
seem to have been a concern of their everyday life.

Still, the intensity of Stein's fascination with Toklas's excreta invites further consideration. The joy she finds in Alice's
"cows" sometimes results in verbal incantations of pleasure
verging on ecstasy:

> Baby precious, yes baby precious
> a movement baby precious a cow
> just out now baby precious,
> all lovely baby precious
> all smelly baby precious,
> all right baby precious
> right out now baby precious . . .
> [2919–9]

At the end of this evocation, mesmerizing in its insistence, "cow" and "baby precious" herself become synonymous:
"and now baby precious a baby / precious our baby precious,
now / baby precious out baby precious of baby / precious"
[2919–9].

Alice's "movements" seem to fulfill a deeply primal and
erotic need in Gertrude. In psychological terms, fecal infatua-
tion can relate to the desire to return to and merge with a lost
mother. Stein's mother died when she was in early adoles-
cence, and although she publicly suggested in *The Making of
Americans* that her mother had "no existence," Claudia Roth
Pierpont found in her notebooks a chilling sentence, which
painfully reads: "All stopped after death of mother."[19] Surely
Toklas cared for and protected her "baby" in a demonstrably
maternal way: she coddled, she cooked, she chastised, she

cleaned, she cherished. If, in Toklas, Stein recovered her maternal loss, then the fecal "cows" may have contributed to the remaking of "mother" in a classic case of fetishism or infantile regression.

Stein's critics have made much of her infantile nature. Some have dismissed her literary word play as little more than child's play, and in a certain sense, the "cow" notes epitomize the reason for this skepticism. I say—and I am certain Gertrude and Alice would approve—let such childishness reign. If we are lucky, we find in marriage the physical, emotional, and spiritual gratifications that originally were secured—or not secured—in parent-child relationships in the birth family. Life is made from these satisfactions or lack thereof.

Stein and Toklas's indulgence of the infantile, particularly Stein's admitted eagerness for Toklas's "cows," could be reduced to a kind of sexual pathology. But it wouldn't be the whole story. Such reduction omits the complexity of the couple's eroticism and erases the possibility of embracing its creativity. Stein's admission—made to Toklas without fear of humiliation, even made with lust—and our reading of it in the notes broadens our discussion of the psychodynamics, but more importantly of the pleasures, of the Stein-Toklas relationship. That an uninhibited anality and the rich language of intimacy it provided were erotic components of the marriage is, I think, a testimony to its expressive freedom, not a symptom of its fixation.

Still, psychology and pleasure do not fully unlock the importance of the "cows." At the deepest level, Stein's scatological interests were artistically and ontologically motivated. The notes ask us to take further account—to take what might best be called a phenomenological account—of the fact that Stein's delight in the prospect and evidence of Alice's "cows" was excessive, even obsessive. It has been said often of Stein's art that she wrote from a fascination with the concrete, the physical. In his introductory essay for Carl Van Vechten's *Selected Writings of Gertrude Stein* (1962), F. W. Dupee remarked on "her insistence on the primacy of phenomena over ideas, of the sheer magnificence of unmediated reality."[20] In *The Autobiography of Alice B. Toklas,* Stein herself explains, "Gertrude Stein, in her work, had always been possessed by the intellectual passion for exactitude in the description of inner and outer reality."[21] As well, she had always been possessed by what she once described in *Everybody's Autobiography* as her compelling interest in "the bottom nature" of people, the nature of repeated behaviors that make us the same and different.[22] Can it be said that the "bottom nature," the "inner and outer reality" that drove Stein's "intellectual passion," was emblematized and most profoundly manifested in the "cow" that came out "gently / primly and completely" [2920–46] from Alice's "darling little bottom" [2925–36]?

Clearly, as the notes help to show, Stein's art was rooted in the steady, ongoing power of a sexual eroticism that found expression in many kinds of physical phenomena—making love, eating, sleeping—repeated and repeated again. If Alice's defecatory "cows," and their "regularity," had a place in the domestic and erotic scheme of the marriage, they were conceivably also a source of inspiration for Stein's dedication to the concrete and to the artfulness of repetition—the rhythmic reiteration of words, phrases, themes—in her life's work. She defined repetition as "insistence," and one would have to concede that defecation is an ultimate, most natural, and most inevitably "insistent" kind of repetition. Perhaps "cows" can't be orgasms because female orgasm is often elusive and irregular; it can't be counted on. In contrast, defecation daily repeats a compulsory sign of living, of being; it is insistent in its pure expression.

For Gertrude Stein the phenomenon of being and her reason for writing—her pure expression—were physical, material, and ultimately of the body. Toklas's excreta were a profound sign of being: Alice's being, Gertrude's being, their being, and being itself—all were mixed and merged in the symbol and the reality of the fecal "cow." This inextricable confluence is asserted in Stein's dictum: "His cow will / make her cow" [2921–2].

"His cow" is in one sense Stein's own sympathetic bowel movement, but it is also, in another sense, herself and her writing. I would suggest that in its unpunctuated, uninterrupted rhythms Stein's writing approaches the mechanics of excretion. Even in content, certain of Stein's works are illumined by the excretory point of view. Line by line, "Lifting Belly" could be read as a paean to the erotic delights and effects of giving—whether actually or artistically—an enema.

In whatever erotic way Stein intended them to be understood, whether implicitly as orgasms in her writings or explicitly as feces in her notes to Alice, "cows" are signs of the physicality of love; they are signs of fusion, and they are, as Ulla Dydo decrees, crucially linked to the act and art of Stein's writing. In her introductory notes to "As A Wife Has A Cow A Love Story," Dydo quite rightly remarks: "In this fact, [of a wife having a cow,] not in any theory, is the key to the life and work of Gertrude Stein. As making love concludes with the cow, so writing concludes with a book. Sexuality and writing become one."[23] Gertrude's devotion to Alice's "cows"—her thoughts about them, her identification with them, her written "treatments" to produce them—combines a heightened and freely discursive eroticism with the desire to make art.

Gertrude Stein / Note #2921–3.

Both in lovemaking and in defecating—and in other erotic realms as well—Toklas's body provided the sensual, corporeal model, the "site of composition" for Stein's ingenious *écriture féminine,* her language of the female rectum and the vagina, her writing pushed out on the page in all its rhythmic, repetitive, regressive and erotic glory.

As her best critics and advocates have discovered, contradictions, oppositions, and ambiguities are at play throughout Stein's life and work. "Cows" are a special case of the ambiguous, and more—much more—could be said speculatively about their meaning as it is revealed in the notes. All speculation aside, in the end Stein and Toklas's notes to each other testify unimpeachably—inarguably—to the love shared by Gertrude Stein and Alice B. Toklas. Theirs was a marriage of total immersion in each other. Quite simply, Alice said, "We entwine" [2921–5b]. And Gertrude concurred: "Baby we is one / Baby we are so happy to be one" [2920–33]. In the happiness of being one, Gertrude and Alice created a unique blend of the conjugal, the erotic, the domestic, and the artistic. Still, they achieved this whole while maintaining separate identities: "she is not / my twin she is my all" [2928–10]. They achieved the most that marriage can offer: in being husband and wife they linked opposites in a resolution, an "all" that was theirs and theirs alone.

The alliance and affection—the marriage—between Gertrude and Alice was truly their religion. More than anything else in the notes—more than the sex, more than the discovery of the fecal "cows," more than the touching sentiment of mundane detail or the playful repartee of Mr. and Mrs. Cuddlewuddle—what moved me was the blessing which, over and over again, Stein, like a god, gave to Toklas and to their union:

> . . . she is so good to me tears come into
> my eyes when I think how good she is to
> me bless you my sweet, bless you, I do know
> how good my baby is to me so sweet so loving
> so forbearing so wonderful oh bless you
> sweet baby every inch of you sweet baby . . .
> [2922–47]

And in this example, the benediction approves the marriage: "bless she bless she / bless she she and / her cow and her husband / all loving" [2919–11].

Stein once pronounced, "It is to be certain that love is lord of all."[24] Her belief in this maxim resonates in the refrain of blessing heard throughout the notes. It is the nuptial song sung against the odds, against propriety, even against history. The marriage sacrament is denied—and has for centuries been denied—to lesbians and gay men. Yet such denial was impossible for these two women, secular Jewish, lesbian lovers who lived in a time when they could have been deported—or, in the extreme, killed—for either of these identities. Liturgically cadent in their insistence on the power of love, Stein's notes assert the couple's unperturbed and enviably self-determined sacrament of marriage, their own particular and daring reconciliation of the two into one: "and baby precious baby / dear it is not queer that I love her here / here in my heart in me all through / and I am in she my baby jew bless / you my sweet" [2928–5].

Questions of love, questions of sex, questions of marriage: these questions have been asked and pondered and answered and asked again in the long history of humankind. That long history has resulted in countless matings, each given the opportunity by fate to create one out of two, to absolve difference in favor of "likeness to loving," to repeat again and again the desire that is both bounded and freed by domesticity.

We often turn to the marriages of others—familial, fictional, biographical—to answer our own need to know what makes a marriage. How does it work? What makes it last, if in fact it does? Near the end of her life, in the libretto for "The Mother of Us All," about the life of feminist Susan B. Anthony,

Stein at 27, rue de Fleurus.

Stein herself posed the age-old questions for us this way: "What is marriage, is marriage protection or religion, is marriage renunciation or abundance, is marriage a stepping-stone or an end. What is marriage."[25]

Gertrude Stein and Alice B. Toklas found the answers to these questions in their own union, and wrote the answers in their notes to each other. Alice—so rightly—called these notes a "beautiful form of literature." They teach us something profoundly beautiful about the art of marriage.

A Word to the Reader

The following information regards selection, editing, and presentation of the notes for this volume. I hope that a complete and fully annotated volume of the notes might someday be published. For this selection I have chosen examples that typify the range of the collection. All the notes presented in the body of this book are complete. However, notes quoted in the introduction are usually given in part, and not all of them are presented in the main text. All renderings of the notes faithfully retain Stein's and Toklas's original lineation. I have not corrected spelling mistakes, the use of British forms, or punctuation discrepancies, even where they were obvious. For example, readers will find that Stein often spells "loving" as "loveing," that "idolize" is written with a British "s" instead of "z," that "cherished" is "chereshed," and that both Toklas and Stein occasionally omit apostrophe marks in contractions such as "I'll" or "we'll." On occasion, commas and periods are difficult to distinguish. Where this has been the case, I have followed the sense of the note. Stein's and Toklas's handwritings are at times difficult to decipher. To insure accuracy, in every case the notes published here have been reviewed and read several times over with Beinecke archivist Timothy G. Young.

Because no dates are given on the notes, there was no way to present them chronologically. Instead, I have ordered them by folder and letter numbers as they are archived under the Beinecke Library's designation YCAL MSS 76, Box 133, Folder Numbers 2918–2929. Folders 2918–2928 contain Stein's notes;

Folder 2929 contains Toklas's. The only exceptions are two of Toklas's notes (2921–5b and 2921–7), which for this volume are captured in with my selections from Toklas Folder 2929. Mr. Young relates that the notes came to Yale in a single folder, loosely arranged, and had passed through several hands before 1995, when he took on the task of analyzing them and giving them their current organization. On the basis of content, handwriting, type of paper, use of pen or pencil, and so on, he grouped, as well as he could, notes that seemed to belong together and could have been written around the same time. About half the notes still retain their original order as found in the single folder. In a few cases, Young has assigned approximate dates based on information in the content of certain notes that matches known events in the couple's life. For example, the very first note in the collection [2918–1] concerns their honeymoon and is written on hotel stationery from London, where they stayed in 1914. As they remain tentative in most cases, Mr. Young's dates are not cited in this publication.

The reading of certain notes is helped by the following comments. Notes 2921–5a (Stein) and 2921–5b (Toklas) indicate two notes originally written on the front and back of the same piece of paper. Stein's Note 2920–18 was written in pen, with a later addendum in pencil. For clarity, the addendum is published in brackets, although Stein did not use them in the original. Toklas's Note 2929–2 begins with a greeting in French, which translates "Best wishes from your wife / from the United States." In the same note, Toklas likely dropped the apostrophe in the contraction "We'll" in the second to the last line.

Illustrations for this volume include selected reproductions of the actual notes, photographs of Stein and Toklas at their various homes, and photo replicas of their household ephemera, such as receipts and identification papers. On a number of her notes, Stein drew simple sketches of round, smiling figures she identified as the "cuddlewuddles," an affectionate name she and Toklas used to describe themselves. Examples of these figures are reproduced on the book cover and in the reproduction of Note 2922–33. Toklas's Note 2929–2, reproduced in this volume, is illustrated with her minute drawings of hearts and flowers. The title of this book is taken from the opening line of Note 2920–24.

Notes

1. Stein, 1922[1968]:380, 381.

2. Nestle, 1987:100.

3. Souhami, 1991:13.

4. Steward, 1984:56.

5. Personal communication with Timothy G. Young, archivist, Beinecke Rare Book and Manuscript Library, Yale University.

6. Personal communication with Timothy G. Young. Also see Gallup, 1947.

7. Stein, 1940:38.

8. Stein, quoting from *The Making of Americans* in her lecture "The Gradual Making of The Making of Americans"; in Van Vechten, 1990:243–44.

9. Ibid., 244.

10. Benstock, 1986:190.

11. Meese, 1992:74–75.

12. Grahn, 1989:11.

13. Bornstein, 1995:138.

14. Stein, 1934; in Dydo, 1993:147.

15. Stein, 1945:21.

16. Stein, 1926; in Dydo, 1993:462.

17. Yeats, 1940:298.

18. Haas, 1973:78.

19. Pierpont, 1998:82.

20. Dupee, in Van Vechten, 1990:xvi.

21. Stein, 1933[1983]:228.

22. Stein 1938; in Hobhouse, 1989:50–51.

23. Dydo, 1993:451.

24. Stein, 1931[1973]:28.

25. Stein, in Van Vechten, 1949[1995]:74.

Works Cited and
Suggestions for Further Reading

Benstock, Shari. *Women of the Left Bank: Paris, 1900–1940.* Austin: University of Texas Press, 1986.

Bornstein, Kate. *Gender Outlaw.* New York: Vintage Books, 1995.

Bridgman, Richard. *Gertrude Stein in Pieces.* New York: Oxford University Press, 1970.

DeKoven, Marianne. *A Different Language: Gertrude Stein's Experimental Writing.* Madison: University of Wisconsin Press, 1983.

Dydo, Ulla E., ed. *A Stein Reader.* Evanston, Ill.: Northwestern University Press, 1993. (Includes "Play" and "As A Wife Has A Cow A Love Story.")

Gallup, Donald Clifford. "The Gertrude Stein Collection." *Yale University Library Gazette,* October 1947, pp. 21–32.

Grahn, Judy. *Really Reading Gertrude Stein.* Freedom, Calif.: The Crossing Press, 1989.

Haas, Robert Bartlett, ed. *Reflection on the Atomic Bomb, Volume I of the Previously Uncollected Writings of Gertrude Stein.* Los Angeles: Black Sparrow Press, 1973. (Includes "Vacation in Brittany.")

Hobhouse, Janet. *Everybody Who Was Anybody: A Biography of Gertrude Stein.* New York: Doubleday, 1989.

Kennedy, J. Gerald. *Imagining Paris: Exile, Writing, and American Identity.* New Haven: Yale University Press, 1993.

Kostelanetz, Richard, ed. *The Yale Gertrude Stein.* New Haven: Yale University Press, 1980.

Meese, Elizabeth. "Gertrude Stein and Me: A Revolution in the Letter." In *(Sem)Erotics Theorizing Lesbian: Writing.* New York: New York University Press, 1992.

Nestle, Joan. *A Restricted Country.* Ithaca, N.Y.: Firebrand Books, 1987.

Newton, Esther. "Alice-Hunting." In *Butch / Femme: Inside Lesbian Gender.* Sally Munt, ed. London: Cassell, 1998.

Pierpont, Claudia Roth. "The Mother of Confusion." *The New Yorker,* May 11, 1998.

Simon, Linda. *The Biography of Alice B. Toklas.* Garden City, N.Y.: Doubleday & Co., 1977. (See especially her "Appendix: An Annotated Gertrude

Stein," which provides a wealth of information linking Stein's works to her relationship with Toklas.)

Souhami, Diana. *Gertrude and Alice*. San Francisco: Pandora/HarperCollins, 1991.

Stein, Gertrude. *As Fine As Melanctha* (1914–1930). Vol. 4 of the Yale Edition. New Haven: Yale University Press, 1954.

———. *The Autobiography of Alice B. Toklas*. London: The Bodley Head, 1933. (Reprint, New York: Penguin Books, 1983.)

———. *Bee Time Vine and Other Pieces* (1913–1927). Preface by Virgil Thomson. New Haven: Yale University Press, 1953.

———. *A Book Concluding With As A Wife Has A Cow A Love Story*. Paris: Editions de la Galérie Simon, 1926.

———. *Everybody's Autobiography*. London: William Heinemann, 1938.

———. *How To Write*. Paris: Plain Edition, 1931. (Reprint, New York: Something Else Press, 1973.)

———. "If You Had Three Husbands" and "Pink Melon Joy." In *Geography and Plays*. Boston: Four Seas Company, 1922. (Reprint, New York: Something Else Press, 1968.)

———. *Lifting Belly*. Rebecca Mark, ed. Tallahassee, Fla.: The Naiad Press, 1989. (First published in *Bee Time Vine and Other Pieces* (1913–1927), 1953.)

———. *The Making of Americans*. New York: Harcourt Brace, 1934.

———. *Paris France*. New York: Scribners, 1940.

———. "Play." In *Portraits and Prayers*. New York: Random House, 1934.

———. *Wars I Have Seen*. New York: Random House, 1945.

———. *The Yale Edition of the Unpublished Writings of Gertrude Stein*. 8 vols. New Haven: Yale University Press, 1951–1958.

Steward, Samuel M. *Dear Sammy: Letters from Gertrude Stein and Alice B. Toklas*. New York: St. Martin's Press, 1984.

Stimpson, Catherine R. "Gertrice/Altrude: Stein, Toklas, and the Paradox of the Happy Marriage." In *Mothering the Mind: Twelve Studies of Writers and Their Silent Partners*. Ruth Perry and Martine Watson Brownley, eds. New York: Holmes and Meier, 1984.

———. "The Somograms of Gertrude Stein." In *The Female Body in Western Culture*. Susan Suleiman, ed. Cambridge, Mass.: Harvard University Press, 1986.

Toklas, Alice B. *The Alice B. Toklas Cookbook*. New York: Harper & Row, 1984.

———. *Staying on Alone: Letters of Alice B. Toklas*. Edward Burns, ed. New York: Liveright, 1973.

———. *What Is Remembered*. New York: Holt, Rinehart & Winston, 1963.

Van Vechten, Carl, ed. *Last Operas and Plays.* New York: Rinehart, 1949.
(New edition: Baltimore: Johns Hopkins University Press, 1995); includes "The Mother of Us All."
————. *Selected Writings of Gertrude Stein.* New York: Vintage Books, 1990
(originally published in different form in 1946; this edition originally
published in 1962).
Weiss, Andrea. *Paris Was a Woman: Portraits from the Left Bank.* San Francisco: HarperSanFrancisco, 1995.
Yeats, William Butler. *Collected Poems.* New York: Macmillan, 1940.

From

Gertrude Stein

to

Alice B. Toklas

My dear wife

      Here we are in London on our honey
moon and we saw the moon and we
said it was the most beautiful and
the most xtraordinary moon that we
had ever seen, thanks for the
moon and thanks for the honey-moon,
which is our moon and which is our honey-moon

Y.D.

[2918–1]

Preciousness, Precious I kiss precious
preciousness which is my darling and my
delight, my sweet baby deliciously
bright bless her I am all sleepy
bless her precious baby precious precious
baby my delight, I kiss her
I am all hers, all hers,

Y.D.

[2918–6]

An incredible sweet wife loved by an incredibly
loving husband.
He walked up and down and he did not frown
Not once.
He treated his wifey to have a cow now
At once.
That is what he did.
And now his eyes are closed with sleepiness,
And love of his wifey,

                                        Y.D.

[2918–8]

Do you really think I would yes I would and
I do love all you with all me.
Do you really think I could, yes I could
yes I would love all you with all me.
Do you really think I should yes I should
love all you with all me yes I should
yes I could yes I would.
Do you really think I do love all you
with all me yes I do love all you with all
me And bless my baby   Y.D.

[2918–17]

Dearest Baby,

    I am watching over you and incidentally
sawing wood, I am watching over you and
incidentally loving you with all my heart
and all me, I am watching over you
and incidentally I am every bit yours
every least little bit yours, I am watching
over you and having you sleep long
and well and wake up all rested, I am
watching over you and incidentally I am
               your hubby.

                           Y.D.

[2918–18]

*Toklas, Stein,
and Basket in
Paris at the
end of World
War II, c. 1944
or 1945.*

Baby, specializing in baby, that is what I am,
Everybody has their specialty and I am
specializing in baby,
Bless baby dear baby all baby and I am
I am specializing in baby splendid
baby rested baby darling baby I am
specializing in my baby god bless her,
be all rested.

                                    Y.D.

[2918–19]

A Poem to Baby precious

Baby looked so pretty with a big hat on
lovely black hair,
Baby looked so pretty with no hat on
lovely black hair,
Baby looks so pretty with its little head
and its lovely black hair sleeping sweetly
on its hard pillow,
Baby looks so lovely, precious baby, baby
looks so lovely precious precious baby

                                Y.D.

[2918–20]

Baby precious has a
cow baby precious now
has a cow baby precious
oh baby precious has
a precious cow now
how well how just
as how as can be
just as now as can
be baby precious has
a cow baby precious
now bless baby precious
and her cow

[2919–6]

With the clothes warm and
tight at the feet of us
all night when baby wakes
all warm she'll be and
never a tickle in her throat
has she not any nothing but
sweet breath coming softly
and sweetly fine from my little
baby she all my wifey

Y.D.

[2919–13]

When all is told lovely
baby precious does not
mind the cold, when
little hubby surrounds
her warm, the cold
cannot do her harm,
bless the baby yes
she says it is it
is nice and warm
and I will he hold
and I will not be
cold and little
hubby will do
what he is told
by little wifey who
is not cold, who
knows the cold is
warm and will do
her no harm bless
her   Y.D.

[2919–14]

Dear dainty delicious darling, dear
sweet selected sovereign of my soul
dear beloved baby dear everything
to me when this you see you will
have slept long and will be warm
and completely tenderly loved by
me dear wifey, precious baby

Y.D.

[2920–2]

Baby precious I have decided that my
baby is more to me than me native
land or anything and I must not
upset me which is to upset she
not for anything and so baby can see
that I will not upset he because
that is to upset she, and little she
and little me must not upset she
which is what is and what is is that
baby precious is the dearest sweetest ownliest
baby precious and I am her own hubby

Y.D.

I worked me wifey   Y.D.

[2920–5]

58

Baby precious, oh dear baby so precious, sweet
kissed baby so precious, lovely precious,
every minute every second more precious,
more baby more precious. Precious. I been all
through your desk so you do not have to
worry about that, and I did not find the ticket,

[I found the ticket in your bag and I have put it]

so you do not have to worry about that, bless

[with mine down-stairs, so everything is found]

my baby precious, my baby precious is so

[and my baby is my love my sweet delight.]

precious she does not have to worry about
that because I can never lose my baby precious
because I hold her so tight and I
love her with all my might and she
is my sweet my neat my lovely treat
my baby precious

Y.D.

[2920–18]

Baby precious I did not mean to
be anything but love and kisses to my
birdie, and I did not mean to shove
the sweet along to bed too quickly I just
meant to be the only loving husband in the
world to the only precious baby in the world,
bless her sweet delight and I love her so
tight bless the sweet precious bless her
I say bless her night and day asleep and awake
sitting by the fire or making cake bless her
bless the sweet my sweet my all sweet

Y.D.

[2920–22]

Baby precious you know baby you are
my precious you know how precious
you are you are all precious and you
know baby you are the only precious the
precious only precious to your hubby,
bless the baby precious all precious all
all precious every bit precious and always
precious to her hubby

Y.D.

[2920–23]

Receipt for purchase of Remington typewriter, dated April 11, 1931.

Baby precious always shines full
of love and dove, baby precious very
sweet is always a treat, baby precious
which I love is sleeping sweetly above
and now I will get in beside her and
shove the hotties too near and then it
will be queer to hear baby say so, bless
baby dear, sweet darling dear my
dear wifey

Y.D.

[2920–24]

My love my love, I love my love,
My love I love, I love my love,
Bless her, her little finger and her
big finger and her whole hand and all
of her bless her, I love my love bless
her and the two little apples inside her
bless her, and the cow that comes out
of her, bless her, I love my love, my
love I love, bless her.

[2920–26]

My baby precious, you feel all treated
treated to have a complete and an entire
cow, yes sweetie you will bless you I
am so full of tenderness and delight in
my blessed wifie that it must overflow
in a cow out of she, there is no
other way to be, oh my blessed
I love you so I love you so from
top to toe, blessed baby

Y.D.

[2920–30]

64

Baby we is one
Baby we are so happy to be one,
Baby baby is precious oh so precious,
Baby, Love and delight is loved with all our
                might,
Baby is to have a sweet cow, a strong cow
        a nice cow a real cow, not a milk
        cow but a splash cow and now,
Baby is so sweet so dear so pure so lovely
        and mine and I am thine

                        Y.D.

[2920–33]

65

Baby precious, I can't write
such pretty poetry as baby precious
but I can love baby as much
as baby precious loves me, yes
it is true my sweet joy and
pride and my lovely bride
and everything else beside
and thank you for a happy
birthday and I worked a little
too and thank you dear baby
precious your dear

                          Y.D.

[2920–37]

Baby precious, its awful cold but
not so cold that I am not treating
and loveing my baby wife, my precious
darling sweet desirable baby wife, and
she needs me and I need she and we
are as loving as loving can be bless she,
bless my baby precious my joy and my
delight and I love her with all my might,
a cow ahoy, a cow now sweet smelly and complete
my baby mate, my sweet

Y.D.

[2920–38]

Baby precious, hubby is very
sleepy, he worked a little
and he loved a lot, what,
his blessed baby wifey thats
what, blessed baby wifey,
a lovely lot, bless her
the blessed baby

                    Y.D.

[2920–40]

Baby precious I write with my baby's
pen but it makes blots and
so I will take a pencil to
tell my beloved my belovee
my blessed beloved how I love
her bless the sweet the dear
the tender the nicely heavy
on the knee beloved how I love her
bless my baby

Y.D.

[2920–44]

Baby precious dear sweet baby precious, I
cleaned up and oiled your scissors,
and so was a little useful, I loved and love
baby terrifically and so is a little
useful and I treated and treat
baby to be oh so very well and
careful and so I am a little
useful, bless my baby bless my
baby she will use me every way
for she every every way for she
bless she

Y.D.

[2920–45]

Baby precious, you are now my baby precious
the precious of a good hubby, who by his faithful
treatment of his dear wifey, his baby precious,
makes her have a nice cow come out gently
primly and completely and then baby precious
will be all rested and everything will
be just right and baby precious will be all
bright and little hubby will be filled with
delight, oh my baby precious I love adore
and idolise you all through, baby precious
all yours hubby

Y.D.

[2920–46]

I am treating my baby precious
so hard so hard not to have
anything the matter with she,
bless her. I am writing an introduction
to her this is to introduce my baby
precious to her baby precious and this
is to introduce her baby precious to his
baby precious, but they being all one
they do not need any introducing bless
the baby precious she is all to me

Y.D.

[2920–47]

72

Little darling little sweet
little joy I entreat
that you meet on your
seat little subject
at your feet little
knees little bleat
Twill not freeze but
come complete sweet
a cow, (<u>not</u> goats) a cow
a cow now.

[2921–1]

Little pinky she, she is my sheeny,
She shines so bright and sleeps so
tight and to-morrow night
she will sleep tight and
to-morrow morning she will be
longing for what for a kiss oh yes
but also for a cow oh how she
will be longing for a cow and
if she keeps so sweet and
she will she will keep this
sheet she will and little
hubby will be will be will
give her with all his
might what so light
not tight but loose
for his goose a cow
like what how like the
kind made in the stables
now not by the sow but
by the cow. His cow will
make her cow.   Y.D.

[2921–2]

74

Dear Mrs.
I take my pen in hand to congratulate
you dear Mrs. on the extremely promising
husband you have. He promises everything
and he means it too. He did not not
mean it. He means it. The darling. This
ejaculation refers to Mrs. not to Mr.
as might be erroneously supposed.
Mrs. is the fountain of all good
all beauty and all sweetness. Mrs.
is a graceful fountain and she
plays over Mr. who is certain that
Mrs. is a grateful fountain which
means that it is grateful to
Mr. to have Mrs. play over him. Mr.
is so grateful. Dear Mrs. Lovingly yours
                                    Mr.

[2921–3]

My only baby Caesars I love
so sweetly now,
My only baby Caesars you
will surely make a cow.
My only baby Caesars
I cherish you this
way. My only baby
Caesars will make a
cow to-day, we say.

Y.D.

[2921–4]

My dearest wife,

This little pen which
belongs to you loves to be
written by me for you, its
never in a stew nor are
you my sweet ecstacy,

Y.D.

[2921–5a]

Dear Mrs.
   To be found.
      Close inside Mr.
         Also a cow to be found
      in baby achieved by Mr. and Mrs.

[2921–6]

Little fool little stool little
fool for me. Little stool little
fool little stool for me. And
what is a stool. That was
the elegant name for a cow.
Little stool little fool little
fool for me. Little fool
little stool for me. And
what is a little fool. A little
fool is an elegant name for
Mrs. C.

                         Y.D.

[2921–8]

Little daisy dot sat behind
a trot a trotting horsey and
where is husband here he is
sadly waiting for little bossy.
And what will she say
when they kiss to-day
she will say he is a good
little boysy. Sweetest
tender neat I love you
to your feet. sweet little
mosey which is short for morsel.

                    Y.D.

[2921–9]

Let us let us conscience
Let us let us conscientiously
rename the sense of
reticence and the
sense of horsey. Horsey
and Flersy and really
little sweet. Really
little sweet to me
little my meat and a cow
now. that is to-morrow
                              Y.D.

[2921–11]

Sitting in her little chair,
Knitting every one a pair,
Doing always her own share
And loving dearly,
Is my baby sweet to me
And what can he say
Clearly, he can say
that he will see, to it,
that she will have
a cow come through
it. Come through what
Caesars on the trot.
She will read the
other too and together
they will come
true, the Caesars and
you, my sweet

                    Y.D.

[2921–12]

82

As surely as Life publishes
me and we get material
and baby has a cow so
surely will the allies
win. You think so.

[2921–14]

With a blue note book.
And a red pencil.
I speak to baby.
I speak to little stomach
I counsel mister to be good.
I suggest kisses
To speak quickly.
And what do I say to
Petunia. Oh Peetunia

                    Y.D.

[2921–15]

Baby is hot.
A hot little sacrifice.
For a husband who was chilly.
But is now warm and frilly.
Frilly as to temper is he
But his wifey oh his wifey is good
And she is wooed.
By hubby as food and indeed
as everything. God bless my baby

[2921–16]

Baby is hot.
So she will sit on the pot.
Only she stands
With the pot in her hands.
And what does her little face do.
It nods.
Can you see a sea.
Not unless from the shore.
We love baby.
I do not say this especially.

[2921–17]

Baby precious you took
little husband so sweetly
through his troubles the way
you always do baby precious
and now hubby is going
to take wifey sweet
baby precious he is all
well and going to take
care of his own dear darling
sweet lovely tender blessed
wifey baby precious

                    Y.D.

[2922–3]

Baby precious, I love Baby Precious with all my
heart and with all my soul and with all my
might, baby precious and a little spider just
went over the paper while I was writing
and a spider at night makes everything
bright, baby precious and it was an
active little spider and my baby is
all bright and all right and all
loved with hubby's all might,
bless baby precious and she is kissed
so sweet from her head to her
feet, baby precious

                              Y.D.

[2922–16]

Baby precious, little sleepy little
wife little sleepy all my life,
Little sleepy is my wife and
little sleepy is hubby to be like
his wife, bless the wife little
hubby can say and he can say
it everyday and every night
and that is all he has to say,
bless the baby the precious tender
loveing lovely loved baby wifey

                              Y.D.

[2922–17]

89

Beloved baby I worked a little
loveing my beloved every second
loveing her oh so lovingly, loveing
her with all of me oh my dear
wife how devoted I am to my
blessed baby and when I am uncomfortable
for my blessed baby it is only because
I do so love to be comforted by my
blessed baby oh the sweet the
sweet sweet sweet bless her

Y.D.

[2922–20]

Baby as precious, as precious
as precious can be, baby precious,
dear sweet delight, I love you tight,
I wish I was always good just as
I am my baby's daily food, I wish
I was as good as she but bless the
precious baby that cannot be because
she is so good so good to me bless
the baby the sweet precious baby all
for me and I am all for she, god
bless my baby my love my life my all
and a lovely ball, oh bless you wifey
am treating you every second wifey dear. here   Y.D.

[2922–23]

91

Baby precious, I been out sawing
and then Basket and me played
and we thought how sweet
our new house was and how
delicious my baby blessed is,
and how we love each other
completely and entirely and
comfortingly, sweet precious

Y.D.

[2922–27]

Just concentrated concentrated on my wife's
cow just concentrated on my wife's cow,
just concentrated and being all concentrated
on my wife's cow my wife will have her
cow now as I am just concentrated
on my wife's cow just concentrated
                    just   Y.D.

[2922–30]

No mistake baby when she is awake no mistake,
she will sleep long, but baby when she is awake
and there is no mistake will have a real
relief, she has belief and I have belief, and
she does know and I know and we both
say so, no mistake, oh bless my baby bless
her cow bless her always and now
concentrate concentrate concentrate.

Y.D.

[2922–32]

Baby sweet Baby sweet cows and
cows baby sweet cows and cows
baby sweet cows and cows and cows

Large smelly cow.

Large smelly cow now now
now how beautifully cow

                    Y.D.

[2922–33]

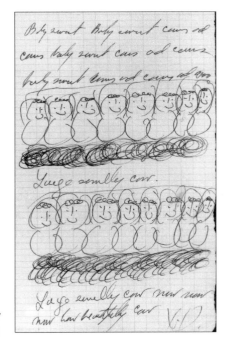

*Gertrude Stein /
Note #2922–33*

95

Little hubling wishes he could be as
stimulating as a cigarette for his wifey
darling but not yet but to-morrow you
bet he will be as stimulating as a
cigarette for his pet and in that
way will after the light of day he
will give the blessed sweetness a cow
to come out, here he is being a cigarette
to his pet, can anything be more contentful
to blessed baby than a nice fat cigarette
you bet and he is it, for his pet you bet
bless her wifey,

Y.D.

a big cow a big cow
a big cow a big cow a big cow
now, I am your cigarette blessed pet.

Y.D.

[2922–37]

Baby precious, it is twelve
o clock, and I am loveing
my wifey and treating her treating
her from top to toe from befront
to behind from left to right
and hugging her tight my
delight, dear dear sweety
all well sweetie mine

                    Y.D.

All the cuddlewuddles are happy because precious baby has
    a cow

[2922–38]

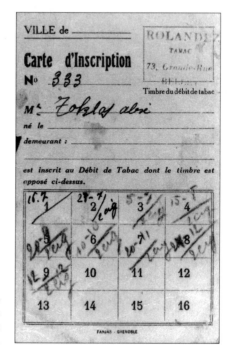

Baby precious, the pen seems to
be writing beautifully and not
blotting at all, I thought it was
because it was not full enough,
I think it blots when it needs filling,
and my baby needs filling with love
every second and she is she is
she is filled up full every
second, and a cow comes out
not every second but nicely every
day, and no pains everywhere and
a good obedient hubby and oh so
lucky bless my lovely wifey

                    Y.D.

[2922–39]

Blessed baby blessed she
All will be well with she.
Tummy soft and cow come out,
No stiffy in my baby stout,
No stiffy in her arms and hands
Only kisses where it softly lands,
Upon her lips her arm and hands,
Blessed baby sweet for me
And all well tenderly

                              Y.D.

[2922–40]

Baby precious, my baby will smoke
me instead of cigarettes and that
will do baby precious just as much
good, baby precious I want to give
baby precious everything she needs
and she only needs me baby precious
and she's got me like the jewish gentleman
said bless my baby precious bless
she

Y.D.

[2922–41]

Baby precious I worked
until I got all quieted
down, and I love my baby,
and we are always happy
together and that is all
that two loveing ones need
my wifey and me

                    Y.D.

[2922–46]

There precious pet I did make
a lot a whole lot and I adored
my wifey every minute and I have
been taking such good care of her
and we will be so good and careful
of each other because we are so loveing
so completely and entirely loveing
and we love each other and that is
all of everything bless my wife
my tenderness my joy without alloy,
bless bless bless she she is all everything
to me

                          Y.D.

[2922–50]

Dear Sweet,
Sweet is sweeter than
peach preserve tomatoe
preserve or honey, Sweet
is sweeter than butter and
money, Sweet is sweeter
than she is funny bless
the Sweet

                    Y.D.

[2923–3]

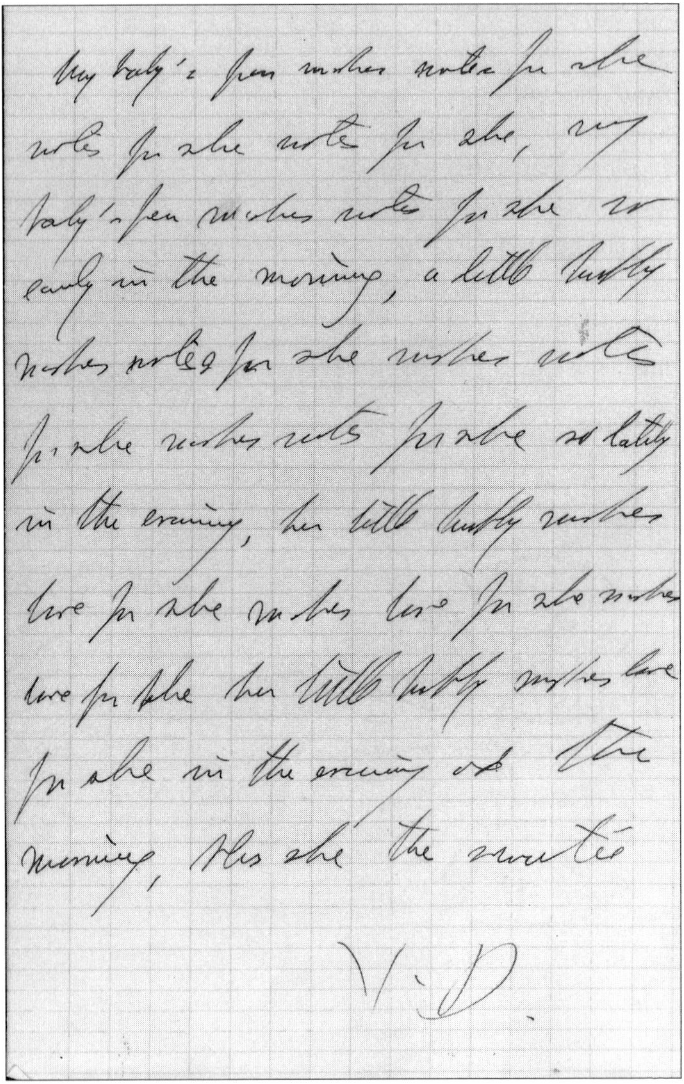

My baby's pen writes notes for she writes for she notes for she, my baby's pen writes notes for she so early in the morning, a little hubby writes notes for she writes notes for she writes notes for she so lately in the evening, her little hubby writes love for she writes love for she writes love for she her little hubby writes love for she in the evening and the morning, Yes she the sweetest

Y.D.

Gertrude Stein / Note # 2923–8

My baby's pen makes notes for she
notes for she notes for she, my
baby's pen makes notes for she so
early in the morning, a little hubby
makes notes for she makes notes
for she makes notes for she so lately
in the evening, her little hubby makes
love for she makes love for she makes
love for she her little hubby makes love
for she in the evening and the
morning, bless she the sweetie

                                        Y.D.

[2923–8]

Dear Baby Precious,

When this you see you know I love but thee,
you are all to me and I am all yours, precious
baby precious just as pretty as pretty can
be and all to me, and I am all she, precious
baby precious always and always all my
baby precious, I love you oh I love you precious
baby precious always precious always more
and more precious my treasure my delight
and I love you with all my might,
baby baby baby precious

                              Y.D.

[2924–2]

The house was just twinkling in the moon light,
And inside it twinkling with delight,
Is my baby bright.
Twinkling with delight in the house twinkling
with the moonlight,
Bless my baby bless my baby bright,
Bless my baby twinkling with delight,
In the house twinkling in the moon light,
Her hubby dear loves to cheer when he thinks
and he always thinks when he knows and he always
knows that his blessed baby wifey is all here and he
is all hers, and sticks to her like burrs, blessed baby

Y.D.

[2924–5]

My these roses smell just like real honey,
But it is my baby that smellest the sweetest for my

money,

Bless the baby, she is so dear to me,
Dear which is dear, which is what she is to me,
Bless the baby, she is sleeping and already,
The cow is ready to come out when she is ready
Bless her the baby, bless her, she is my
baby,   Bless her,

Y.D.

This is a real poem
Just like Chaucer, bless her.

[2924–7]

A Command Poem,

Commanded by wifie, written by hubbie,
who is always commanded by wifie to be wifey's
hubby and he is, would be even if he wasn't
commanded cause he just is but loves to be commanded.

                    Listen to hear
                    Feel it to see
                    Makes it be near
                    Which it is she,
                    Which it is she
                    Inside in me
                    Makes it be on her head
                    Which it is all of her wed
                    Made sure they are tight,
                    Once is a kiss
                    Twice is a kiss
                    Three times and four times
                    Five times and six times
                    All times and more times,
                    Each one is a kiss,
                    There is no miss,
                    It is all kiss
                    Blessed she me
                    Blessed me she
                    Blessed we

                                        Y.D.

[2924–9]

Blessed baby,
I am tired and I am sleepy
and perhaps I have an idea I
am all yoursy

Y.D.

[2924–10]

My dearest sweetness is all better,
My dearest sweetness bless her
My darling my love my delight
And I love her tight, with all my might
Sweetness sweetness my own jelly
belly sweetness is getting better and
better, not a german voice on the radio anywhere
to-night, god bless my sweetness my joy
my pride my wife my life and I am all hers

Y.D.

[2924–13]

My precious, be careful not
to slip on the floor down-
stairs because Basket has been
hunting slabs of butter every
where, oh my baby I love you
so and the butter is slippery my
precious baby is all well precious

Y.D.

[2924–15]

Police citation
given to Stein for
walking her dog
without a muzzle
or leash. Paris,
February 15, 1945.

Baby precious

Will my wifey be all well, yes she will,
Will her hubby make her all well yes he will,
Will she have a cow come out, yes she will
Will she be all well without a doubt, yes she will

Baby precious

Will my wifey know her hubby loves her well, yes she will,
Will she know he is all hers, yes she will
Will she be a happy queen for her little king, yes she will
Will she will she will she be all well yes she will

Dear wifey all   Y.D.

[2924–18]

I use the little goldy pencil
to tell my sweet love she is my
life, I use the little goldy
pencil to tell her I love
but her I love but her she
is all to me god bless
she wifey,

                    Y.D.

[2924–20]

Baby precious my own delight, my
sweet my tender my always right, my
love my wifie, my all and all my sweetest
baby my little ball, my everything always,
my just like that, just everything always,
and always that, my sweetest, my birthday
my Christmas and New Year my only my
darling and always here, my heart your
hubby your chanticlear and all here bless you

Y.D.

[2925–3]

Come all cozy
Smells like a posey
Curl it out straight
Makes it a weight
That is what it is there,
Tickling which is her hair,
How are we tight
Glue is our delight,
What silky,
Yes milky
Dear legs all alright

[2925–5]

Baby precious,

    We came in and we did see all baby's
shawls but baby precious was in her big bed waiting
for her hubbie who adores who loves but she who
is all to she and she is all to he, and it
seems as cold but is it, Basket he jumped
up and down and I walked up and down
and we both thought about our precious
you are my precious and I thought about my
precious, bless my precious and in every way
and everyday I keep her warm, now baby
don't say do you, because I do bless you

                              Y.D.

[2925–6]

My fingers is stiff my love is
strong, my baby is my darling just
right along, god bless my baby
she is all to me there is nobody
anywhere but she, she is me
and I am she and we are as
happy as happy can be

                    Y.D.

[2925–7]

I made so many babies and I am
so sorry I was naughty and I walked
up and down and loved my baby
and I am all hers and she is all
mine precious precious baby

Y.D.

[2925–16]

Baby precious, I cut off ivy off the
terrace, I walked up and down, I
read the bible, I wrote a lot, I loved my
baby, I was all hers and am, and I am
sleepy, and Basket barked and here I am
bless you, bless you sweet dear wifie

Y.D.

[2925–18]

Baby precious
The stars are bright and I love
my baby, I made lots of literature
and I loved my baby I am going to
bed and I love my baby, and I heard
the communique and I love my baby, there
is lots of news but nothing new, and I
love my baby god bless she I love she
I love love love my baby

Y.D.

[2925–19]

*Stein's and Toklas's
authorization/identification
papers permitting specified
travel within France
during World War II.
Dated June 11, 1940.*

Lily bright all my delight,
When she was born for me,
Singing the song of everything
That is what she sings,
She sings to me and she
hears me singing to her
And telling her all her
birthday is me to her,
Give me to her dear sweety,
Give me to her,
On her birthday she has me
and in front and before,
Sweet birthday dear birthday
I am all she for her, sweet
birthday dear birthday sweet
birthday I bore her in my
arms on her sweet birthday
because she is tiny and I
am all for her, blessed
baby sweetly, she is all
a birthday baby for me, blessed
baby sweetly blessed baby,

Y.D.

[2925–22]

122

Baby, sweet baby
Baby my sweet baby,
Baby all baby all my baby,
Baby baby baby, thats what you hear me say,
Baby all my baby all night and all day.
Baby sweet kissed baby, baby sweet baby,
Sweetly sleeping baby, unbathed but delicious
My baby, sweet baby clean baby all baby.
This is what I say, I love her all night and I
love her all day and every day and every night
and in every which way and only she and
all she my sweetie

Y.D.

[2925–23]

There precious pretty, the child's story
is working in nicely with the novel called
Ida and I have been writing pages of
Ida, ain't it nice to write to order god
bless my baby looks so pretty and
gardening is so good for her, god
bless my baby how I love her god
bless my baby

Y.D.

[2925–29]

Baby precious,
>   Sweet oh so sweet,
>   Dear oh so dear
>   Near oh so near
>   Here oh so here
>   Inside oh so inside
>   Wide oh so wide
>   Bride oh so bride
>   Inside oh so inside
>   Bless you baby

>   Y.D.

[2925–30]

I put the pansies away
And they are so pretty and gay
And my sweet baby is prettier and gayer even
than the pansies.
Oh I love you so,
You know I do
Bless you
My sweet I am all yours every bit of
me is yours bless you my sweet sweetie

Y.D.

[2925–31]

Baby precious

     My lips kiss hers and she kisses mine and
her eyes shine and so do mine bless her.
  She is a sweet and happy neat
  Her little nose has a drop which is a treat,
  She has little booties upon her feet
  Really little boots made of wool
  If it is not wool it is cotton
  And she has a darling little bottom.
  Bless baby, bless my wife
  She is all my life

                     Y.D.

[2925–36]

Here is a lovely new note book to
fill full of notes
A lovely new note book to fill
full of hopes,
And notes and hopes and
baby's dotes, I dote on she
She dotes on me, we dote
on each other oui oui oui.

[2925–40]

Everything my baby is is
lovely and wise, little husband
tries and tries to be just
as good as lovely she his wifey
but it is a difficulty because
she is so wonderfully she
and he is only a little he
but he adores her and he is
all hers and he takes care of
her head to which he is wed god
            bless her   Y.D.

[2925–42]

Precious wifey,

All flowers tell me
What a lovely flower is she
lovelier than any flower
can be is she
And I am all hers which makes
her glow because she
knows that it is so.
God bless wifey,
She is a tender page
and every page is open to
me and every page in me
is open to she and such
a sweetie is she such a
sweetie

Y.D.

[2925–45]

Babiest preciousest sweetest adorest, allest
mine and I am allest thine precious baby
mine, it is so sweet of my baby to be always
right and to be always bright and to be
always loved with all my might so
sweet and so tender so dear and so pretty
and so loving and so chereshed and so perfect
and so unutterably tender baby mine all
               thine   Y.D.

[2925–46]

Blessed sweetest baby perfect,
lovely well and rested all, sweetest
dearest only darling lovely enticing
lovely pearl, only angel brightest
love-bird all and always all to
me I do love her with all me,
she is all the world to me, she
is resting bless her bless her darling
sweet heart wifey mine I am all thine

Y.D.

[2925–48]

Dear Blessed wifey

I love you dear blessed wifey
I am all yours dear blessed wifey
I worship you dear blessed wifey,
I idolise you dear blessed wifey,
I want to take care of you dear blessed wifey
I kiss you dear blessed wifey
I kiss you again dear blessed wifey
I kiss you again and again dear blessed wifey
I kiss you again and again and again dear blessed wifey
I just completely and entirely and everlastingly love you dear
blessed wifey

Y.D.

[2925–52]

To my baby on its birthday

My baby is a birdie sitting on a
bough, and the bough is hubby.
My baby is a forget me not, which makes
every bouquet lovely, and her
hubby is the bouquet for his lovey.
My baby is a treasure sitting on
its pleasure, and its pleasure is
its hubby
    Blessed baby on its birthday.

My baby is so beautiful so tender
and so true so feeding full in
the most difficult days the
most lovely and cherished in all
its ways, oh blessed baby, I
just cry when I think how tenderly
you are me and I am thee,
oh baby sweet oh baby dear
oh baby tender oh baby
baby my baby my love my delight
baby my baby I hold you tight.

        Baby on its birthday.
My baby on its birthday is tender
and sweet and true, my baby on its
birthday its hubby is all to you, he
loves you he adores you he is all yours
wifey mine, oh baby I do love you,
I love you all the time and so

much more and so loving, baby my
delight, I love you oh baby blessing
I love you with all my might,
on your birthday and always bless
you oh bless you my wifey,

Y.D.

[2926–1]

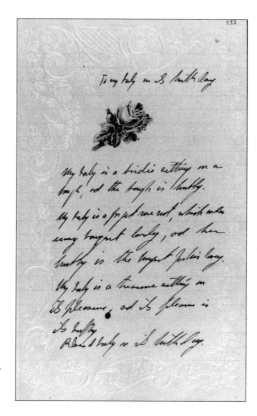

Gertrude Stein /
Note #2926–1,
first page

Baby precious, you is going to have
a lovely movement cow come out just
nicely, and little hubby never means
to be anything but good to his wifey,
and he never means to do anything
but agree with his wifey and he
never means to do anything
but give his wifey a cow right
now, bless she bless she bless she
dear wifey whose hubby is all hers
and adores her and gives her a cow now

Y.D.

[2926–7]

Baby precious,

　　　　There is always the news that
baby is precious my precious all my precious
and that I am all hers, there is
always the news that she is me
and I am she, there is always
the news that she is all to me
and I am all to she, baby precious
baby precious she me, me she,

　　　　　　　　　　Y.D.

[2926–11]

It was a tragedy baby precious, the last
three pages of my novel were torn
out and I never knew the end but I
loved my baby precious just as
preciously and loved her more preciously
and I loved her completely preciously
lovely sweet darling dear baby precious
all here precious baby precious

Y.D.

[2926–14]

Baby precious, you is such a comfort
baby precious such a comforting baby precious
and little hubby is all comforted
by his comforting baby precious,
and now he has worked a little
and he is all sleepy and oh so
loving blessed baby precious
my joy and my delight and I love
her with all my might baby
precious

Y.D.

[2927–1]

Baby precious, I almost did like
my baby precious go to sleep right
there, bless baby precious bless her
with care, bless baby precious bless
her everywhere, asleep in her chair asleep
with her little hubby taking care, to
wake her up and tell her he is so glad
she is there, there everywhere

Y.D.

[2927–3]

Baby precious, the book is really awfully
good and now I am sleepy, and my
baby's full dinner just is
giving her a good cow now
and I love her so, and I am so proud
of her being once more a shopper,
bless her she is my sweet bless
her

Y.D.

[2927–5]

Baby precious, Pepe says it is
time to go to bed and papa precious
says he will, bless baby precious
I did not do nothing much, I
finished reading the ms. and then
I thought I would work but I just
said no I will go to bed and
look at as well as love baby precious
how I love baby precious

Y.D.

[2927–6]

Baby precious,
My delight baby precious she is alright,
Baby precious tender and true baby precious her
little jew is all to you.
Baby precious lovely pet, baby precious
every bet is that my baby precious is
all mine and I am all hers
Bless her

Y.D.

[2927–10]

Baby precious,
　　　　One two three and in all three is
all my love for she baby precious.
Baby precious stars and moons tell my
baby precious husband croons out all
his love for baby precious sweet delight
whom he loves with all his might,
Baby precious

Y.D.

[2927–11]

Blessed baby, We is all sneezing
so quick to bed and chill in little
baby who is so sensibly in bed,
bless her we warm each other she me
I she bless the baby, oh bless her, she
is so sweet oh blessed baby, blessed
baby, Pepe sneezes, we freezes and Baby
pleases, her little hubby all hers.

Y.D.

[2927–12]

Baby precious all my baby precious, I did
right a little and I did love and I do love
and I will love and I shall love my
blessed baby and I treat her to have a
nice cow come out and now I am all
sleepy and all loving and baby is
all warm with her husband's love and her
new shoes and it is not yet New Years
but every New Year is a happy new
year for the Cuddlewuddles bless them my baby
and have a cow come out you little stout now

Y.D.

[2927–15]

Baby precious,

     Yes baby precious little hubby's eyes
is closing because he sawed and then he
pawed over the books he found in a closet
and then he treated his dear wifey to
have her cow come out now that is
to-morrow at eight and he said
dear precious dear precious I am all hers
and she is all mine and it is all fine
dear precious   Y.D.

[2928–1]

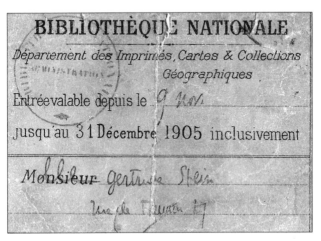

Stein's library card for the Bibliothèque Nationale in Paris. Dated December 31, 1905.

Baby precious, I love you so my precious
my sweet my love my adored one I love
you so precious baby and you will
have a cow again and then again and
always again and baby precious baby
dear it is not queer that I love her here
here in my heart in me all through
and I am in she my baby jew bless
you my sweet I am all her treat and she
is all mine and together we shine brightly

                              Y.D.

[2928–5]

148

Baby precious, I gardened by moonlight,
I adored my wifey, I just completely
and entirely idolised my wifey,
I gave her a good movement, I gave
her love and kisses and now I am
sleepy, and bless my baby bless
her   Y.D.

[2928–6]

Dearest sweetest loveliest and all my baby
is just so little and tall, she is so
fat and neat and thin, she is not
my twin she is my all and lively
like a ball and tender as the
fall and lovely as a wall,
and all and all, bless she and a
wall holds you in and she holds
me in and I hold her in and she is
my win my winsome sweety

Y.D.

[2928–10]

Baby precious, I love you so baby
precious and its a pleasure a complete
and entire pleasure to tell you
so baby precious a complete and
an entire pleasure to tell you
so baby precious sweet sweet baby
precious my own and I am all hers
and all here,

                              Y.D.

[2928–11]

Baby precious, by word of
mouth by kisses by loveing
her flowers and her food
I tell my wifey how I
love her, yes I do,
bless her yes I do
bless her

                    Y.D.

[2928–17]

My dear sweet darling baby, I worked a little
and I loved my wifey lots and lots blessed
baby all flowers and vegetables and
sweetness, and can we order from Richard
in Chambery more more of my candies and
also more candied fruits, but lots of my
candies, and can I tell my baby how much
sweeter she is than any candy bless
the darling bless the darling darling, bless
the sweet, the sweetie

Y.D.

[2928–19]

Writing a poem to my wifey with
my new pencil, dear wifey always new
and fresh finding her way into the
heart of hubby who adores her bless
her, sweet wifey tender wifey lovely
wifey, dear wifey, I love you dear
sweet loving tender wifey I love
but she she is all to me sweet
wifey my wifey and I am all hers
dear dear wifey

                                        Y.D.

[2928–21]

From

Alice B. Toklas

to

Gertrude Stein

My own petsie is a darling
and I love him dearly and
completely and sweetly.

Allie mine
We entwine

[2921–5b]

Alice B. Toklas / Note #2929–2

Baby love
Call your dove.
She's your own
She's not gone
Just quietly waiting
Knowing always she's mating
With her dored own boy

[2921–7]

Les meilleurs voeux de votre femme
      des Etats Unis.

Melly Christmas-hubby dearest
Here we are always nearest.
You've got no peer. you're the peerest
Melly Christmas wifie's good
Hides it under a thick hood
It will be your constant food

Good baby
Is all me
To delight
With all my might
Hubby is my pleasure

Baby boy
You're no toy
But a strong-strong husband
I dont obey
Do this you say
Well do it together and
Thats the way we obey

[2929–2]

158

Dearest Love I'm attending
to the locksmith and I'll
be back soon. Hubby must
not worry but ask Marie
to tell me to come up to
make your coffee. Be
rested and all loving &
know wifie thinks you
are better behavioured
every second & she loves
the behaviours you are
giving her & she will
have more thank you so
much.   Y.W.

[2929–4]

Here's a song for love bird
Resting prettily
Wife's treatment has been heard

Husband's well and cured
Nothing wrong
No more naughty's be endured

Husband is an instantaneous obediencer
He likes to be well
And be hers Mrs. speaks he ups & obeys her

[2929–6]

Sweet
pinky
You made
lots of literature
last night didn't
you. It is very good. I
like this one best. You
are doing most hand-
somely. Would you mind
if I didnt think you a
Post-Impressionist. You
arent lovely.
You
are
not a
cubist either.
It's such very
orderly literature.
Much more so than Pablos.
La Jolie is quite messy
compared to this. You
never were messy-lovie-but
it's more crowded now &
I like it. You can almost
say anything you please
can't you-

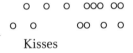

Kisses

[2929–7]

My dearest
Because I didn't say
goodnight and I
miss it so-please know
now how much I love
you-Gertrude dearest.
Good night.

[2929–8]

Dear Mr. Quddlewuddle, How do you ? And will you pleas
accept more of the same every day in every "way more and
more and more and more. Can you suspext how muxh I love you
suspect seems a difficult word to writeM I have just looked
up to see if you were as beautiful as I rememvered and I found
that you were employed with a pencul and paper but not with a
bote , babies get written more hastily than notes, drawings
are done almost as quickly as babies. Thrse are just observa-
tiobs. Notes are a very beautiful form of literature ; they
are never too frequent, do not fear to overwhelm me with the.
H Now the writing has changed, it is has now probably becpme a
eetter to Harry Phelan Gibb R Esquitr. G Y Tè To- dayçs lette
è letter is not perhaps so ibteresting as my last , that may b
be said to be entirely dye to neing Lindoeâ,; if it is less a-
meusing than Mrs. or Mme. Jeanne Cook's that is bexause U am

Alice B. Toklas / Note #2929–9

Dear Mr. Cuddlewuddle, How do you ? And will you pleas
accept more of the same every day in every wway more and
more and more and more. Can you suspext how muxh I love you
suspect seems a difficult word to writeM. I have just looked
up to see if you were as beautiful as I rememvered and I found
that you were employed with a pencul and paper but not with a
bote , babies get written more hastily than notes, drawings
are done almost as quickly as babies. Thrse are just observa-
tiobs. Notes are a very beautiful form of literature   ; they
are never too frequent, do not fear to overwhelm me with the.
H Now the writing has changed, it is has now probably become a
èetter to Harry Phelan Gibb R Esquitr. G Y Tè To- daycs lette
è letter is not perhaps so ibteresting as my last , that may e
be said to be entirely dye to neing Lindoed, ; if it is less a-
meusing than Mrs. or Mme. Jeanne Cook's that is bexause U am

[2929–9]

A happy birthday sweetest happier and
happeir every day., better and better in ever
way, weller and weller every day, fuller of
love I say. This is what we will be having for
my birthday boy, my joy.

DEAR MR. CUDDLE-WUDDLE: To you I addreqq
my confratulationq on capitals, commas, periods,
errors and: and in LOVE.

<u>G</u>

I also present to you my komplete devotion, of wuch you have aeready read and heard but
which you are pleased to read and hear again. A
wife's devotion should always fice plzasure to a
h   husband! But it is nothing compared to a husband
lovem Oj no a husnand's love is like nothing else
in all the world and makes all the happiness of
Mrs. Vuddlewuddlem who hopes however to find maby
ways of giving thr general all the satisdaction he
so greatly , erits. eWill he please axxept all her
love and herself?

[2929–10]

A happy birthday sweetest happier and
happeir every day., better and better in ever
way, weller and weller every day, fuller of
love I say. This is what we will be having for
my birthday boy, my joy.
  DEAR MR. CUDDLE- WUDDLE: To you I addreqq
my confratulationg on capitals, commas, periods,
errors and: and in LOVE.
     G
  I also present to you my komplete devotion, of wuch you hawe abready read and heard but
which you are pleased to read and hear again. A
wife's devotion should always fice plaasure to a
h husband! But it is nothing compared to a husband
lovem Oj no a husnand's love is like nothing else
in all the world and makes all the happiness of
Mrs. Vuddlewuddlem who hopes however to find maby
ways of giving thr general all the satisdaction he
so greatly ,erits. øWill he please axxept all her
love and herself?

P. K.   P.K.

Alice B. Toklas / Note #2929–10

Stein and Toklas with Basket and Pepe
at Bilignin in the mid-1930s.